C000185204

THE AUTHORITY GUIDE TO
PITCHING YOUR
BUSINESS

How to make an impact and be remembered –
in under a minute!

MEL SHERWOOD

Dear Tiffany,
With best wishes
Mel

The Authority Guide to Pitching Your Business
How to make an impact and be remembered – in under a minute!
© Mel Sherwood

ISBN 978-1-912300-02-0
eISBN 978-1-912300-03-7

Published in 2017 by Authority Guides
authorityguides.co.uk

Printed in the United Kingdom.

Contents

A pitch does not take place in the library of the mind; it takes place in the theatre of the heart.

Roger Mavity

Acknowledgements

This book could not have been written without the help and support of a number of people, so my heartfelt thanks go to:

- my parents, Graham and Lauris Sherwood, for the initial proofreading and for being my biggest supporters no matter what my endeavours

- Sue Richardson, Christopher Cudmore and the team at SRA Books for the opportunity to be a part of this series

- my friends and associates in the Professional Speaking Association in Scotland, the UK and beyond for your invaluable support, advice and encouragement

- the enablement team and all the amazing entrepreneurs I met through Entrepreneurial Spark where this journey began

- Renée Philippi, Lorna Slater and Lorna McCallum, my good friends in business and life for providing gentle nudges to keep me focused

- Gordon Craig for providing a keen eye and a fresh perspective on my draft manuscript

- all the #pitchtastic entrepreneurs and business people I have had the privilege to work with in my training courses, masterclasses and one-to-one coaching sessions – your dedication, passion and commitment are my inspiration.

Regardless of the changes in technology, the market for well-crafted messages will always have an audience.

Steve Burnett

Introduction

'What do you do?' is one of the most common questions asked both in a business context and socially, so being able to clearly, confidently and succinctly explain who you are and what you do is fundamental. With people's attention spans becoming shorter, it's crucial to be able to answer the question in a way that is concise, relevant and engaging.

Business people and entrepreneurs risk losing opportunities, credibility and money because they 'pitch' their business badly or they completely avoid chances to speak about what they do. This is especially true if it involves speaking in front of a group of people. In a competitive market, it is important for you to be seen, heard and able to clearly articulate your unique offering and how you differ from your competitors. Anyone you meet could be a potential customer or someone who could help you to grow your business. As first impressions last, it's important to be 'pitch ready' at any given time and able to explain what you do simply and credibly, and in a way that is engaging and memorable (for all the right reasons).

I first started helping people to become what I call '#pitchtastic' after noticing so many business owners doing themselves a disservice when introducing themselves at networking events.

It saddened me to see intelligent, talented, hardworking people struggling to express what they actually did and how they helped their ideal customers... and their businesses were suffering as a result.

To be honest, I struggled with my own pitch when I first set up in business. Despite my background as a performer, which meant I was reasonably comfortable speaking to a room full of strangers, I still struggled with what to say. I'm Australian but I also have that very British mentality about not wanting to brag or to blow my own trumpet for fear of sounding like a show-off or putting people off by appearing 'too confident'. Having said that, I'm also well aware that if I don't sound confident about my business I can't expect anyone else to have any confidence in me.

So I learned everything I could about how to effectively pitch my business and I've developed a winning formula that I have been able to share with thousands of coaching clients and workshop participants. Now I'm delighted to have the opportunity to help even more business people to become #pitchtastic through this book.

Who should read this book?

This book is for you if you are an entrepreneur, a solopreneur, a business owner, a sole trader or anyone in business and:

- you attend networking events or exhibit at trade shows as part of your marketing strategy

- you struggle to clearly and confidently explain what you do when speaking about your business

- you don't feel comfortable speaking in front of a room full of people

- you hate being the centre of attention but know you need to get out and promote yourself in order to succeed in business

- you want to know how to avoid bland, boring waffle and sound clear, confident and credible

- you want to be remembered, recommended and referred in order to generate sales and build your organisation.

It will also be useful if you are employed in a company and find yourself in a role that requires you to speak about what your organisation does. The information and exercises in this book will help you to simplify and clarify your message and confidently communicate it to 1 or 100 people.

It will cover what I call your 'conversational pitch', which is the short answer to the question 'What do you do?', and your 30 to 60-second 'elevator pitch', which is a longer explanation about how your product or service helps your customer. You may have heard an elevator pitch also described as a networking pitch, a magic minute or an elevator speech.

This book focuses primarily on face-to-face communication; however, once you nail your value proposition and incorporate it into your conversational pitch and your 30 to 60-second pitch, you will be able to repeat that consistent message in every element of the communication about your business.

How to use this book

You may choose to read the book from cover to cover, doing the exercises and developing your pitch and your confidence as you progress through the pages. It has been written with this process in mind. However, you may also choose to dip into the relevant chapters depending on your needs. Either way, I hope you find the exercises, templates, tips and techniques helpful as you create and deliver your #pitchtastic pitch.

The best way to develop your pitch making skills is to practise.

Chris Westfall

1. What is a pitch and why do I need one?

The *Oxford English Dictionary* describes a pitch in this context as 'a form of words used when trying to persuade someone to buy or accept something'.

In business, you may be required to deliver a sales pitch, a pitch for funding or investment or even a pitch for a competition. But the most likely requirement and the main focus for this book is for a 30 to 60-second elevator pitch. This type of pitch is widely recognised as a short summary that describes a person, product, service, organisation or event and its value proposition.

Some sources suggest that the phrase 'elevator pitch' was coined during the golden years of Hollywood when a writer would catch an unsuspecting executive in the elevator and pitch an idea for a film in the time it took for the elevator to reach the top floor. Daniel H. Pink tells the story behind what may have been the world's first-ever elevator pitch in his best-selling book, *To Sell is Human: The surprising truth about persuading, convincing and influencing others*. According to Pink, in 1854, Elisha Otis dramatically demonstrated his elevator safety device on the floor of the Crystal Palace Exposition in New York in front of a large audience by ascending in an elevator cradled in an open-sided shaft. Halfway up, he had the hoisting rope cut with an axe.

The platform held fast while the audience gasped. A very persuasive pitch!

Regardless of when the phrase was first used, there will always be times when you will need to pitch your business. Opportunities are everywhere. You never know when you might have the chance to speak with someone who is interested in your product or service, or who knows someone else who would be, so there is a strong argument to be pitch ready at any given time.

Once you are clear on your brand proposition and have developed a concise elevator pitch that you can deliver with confidence, this will form the basis for all of your brand communication and any future pitches. For example, a couple of years ago I helped a client develop a 60-second elevator pitch for her new start-up business. We spent several hours drilling down into exactly how to describe the complex product and identifying the key benefits she wanted to highlight before writing a short script that was easy to remember and easy to say. It took some time to get it right but it was the foundation for a pitch that led her to winning £100,000 in a business funding competition and being offered a further £250,000 worth of investment to grow her start-up. It is worth taking the time to get clear on your message – if you're not clear, it's difficult for anyone else to be!

Should you ditch the pitch and have a conversation?

Some people think the elevator pitch is an out-of-date concept but irrespective of how you go about it, you still have to be able to reply to the question 'What do you do?' or to respond when someone asks, 'Can you tell us a bit about yourself?' A nervous and stumbling answer is not going to fill the questioner with confidence about you or your business. First impressions count and very often answering this question is the first opportunity for someone to get to know you – what impression do you want to give them?

Exercise

Consider the word 'pitch' – what thoughts and feelings come up for you? Are they positive, neutral or negative? How do you think your thoughts and feelings about pitching impact your own pitch?

Many people are uncomfortable with the word 'pitch'; it is often associated with being 'salesy' and a lot of people don't want to appear too salesy, nor do they want to be sold to. Others are uncomfortable with the word because they have had a bad experience of pitching in the past, whether they were unsure what to say or they were not confident in saying it. But when you think about it, life is a pitch. We have been pitching since we were small children – convincing our parents we needed more pocket money, persuading our friends to choose one movie over another or influencing a colleague to our way of thinking.

In my workshops and masterclasses, I often ask participants to discuss the difference between pitching and selling and to decide whether they are the same thing. While there is often a bit of debate around the question, the general conclusion is that the pitch is the start of the conversation and the selling takes place as you build the relationship. The purpose of the pitch is not to sell, but you do need the initial pitch to start the conversation by capturing someone's attention, piquing their interest and making them curious to know more. That is why it's important to be pitch ready at any given time; you never know when you will be asked the question that could spark the conversation that leads to further opportunities.

Don't bombard them though!

It's important to note that the question 'What do you do?' is not necessarily an invitation to bombard the questioner with two minutes of rhetoric about you. In a one-to-one conversation you will most likely answer the question with your conversational pitch, your short 7 to 10 word explanation of what you do, which should ideally lead to further conversation.

If you know what elements of what you do that you want to get across, parts of your pitch can be dropped into the conversation naturally. But if you've never given any thought to how you communicate what you do, or put time into preparing a 30 to 60-second pitch that outlines your value proposition, you may struggle to clearly express yourself.

What are the benefits of a #pitchtastic pitch?

Not only does a great pitch help people to know who you are and what you do, if it is delivered well it will help them to remember you as well as to prospect for you. When your pitch is clear, concise and memorable, if one of your connections then encounters someone with the exact problem you solve, you will be the first person that comes to mind.

Key points

- Every business person needs a pitch.
- First impressions count so it's important to take the time to get your pitch right.
- A clear and confident pitch will help people to remember you and lead to further conversations and opportunities.

2. Pitchfalls – are you making these mistakes?

If you've been to networking events or other corporate events where people are talking about their business, it's likely you will have found yourself warming to some people and not to others. There are various reasons for this but if the talk is about a business that you have no need for or no interest in, there will be some people who still manage to grab your attention and others who don't.

Exercise

Take a moment to think about some elevator pitches you have heard. Which ones were the most memorable? What made them stand out? Did they stand out for the right or wrong reasons?

Pitchfalls that can make a pitch stand out for the wrong reasons

Too much me, me, me

It's important to remember that when someone asks you 'What do you do?', they don't really care about what you do, they care about what you can do for them. But so many business people love to talk about themselves and go on and on and on… and on… about themselves and what they do without any consideration for the people they are communicating with. In any pitch, presentation or even a conversation, the more 'you' language you can include versus 'I' or 'we' language, the more you will be able to engage people.

Features not benefits

Your product or service may have loads of features but your potential customers don't care about them; they only care about the outcome, the result, what's in it for them. Don't harp on about the features; think about the benefits of your product or service and include them in your pitch.

Mumbling

One of the most frustrating things when someone is speaking is the inability to understand them because they mumble. Not only is it difficult to hear what they're saying (which defeats the point of the communication), but a mumbler also gives the impression that they don't really care about what they are saying, or whether their audience hears and understands them.

Unclear and/or confusing

In my line of work, I hear a lot of pitches. Sometimes when I first start working with someone I will hear the same pitch several times. Sometimes I still don't understand it even after hearing it more than once. Even if your product or service is complicated, in fact especially if your product or service is complicated, you need to make the time and effort to break it down to ensure it is simple and easy to understand.

Too much information

Providing too much information about what you actually do is boring and often irrelevant. I can't tell you the amount of times I've heard a pitch along the lines of 'Hello, my name is X and my company is Y. We do blah, blah, blah… and we also do blah, blah, blah… and we do a bit of blah, blah, blah…' I've also heard pitches where people were trying to speak about several different businesses in one 60-second pitch, which, apart from leaving me completely confused about what they wanted me to do with that information, sounded a bit desperate!

Waffling/rambling/long-winded

'Some people don't have much to say but you have to listen a long time to find out.' This quote from *The Perfect Presentation* by Andrew Leigh and Michael Maynard sums it up perfectly. It's really annoying when people seem to talk without a point; it makes it very difficult to follow and most people switch off. Know your point and get to it quickly.

Irrelevant

A pitch will never create the impact you desire if it is not meaningful to the person or people you are communicating to. When you are thinking about how you describe who you are and what you do, you need to consider your audience – what they might be interested in and how your product or service will be relevant to them or someone they know.

No story

People don't remember facts and figures but they do remember stories. We have been telling stories and listening to stories for centuries; a relevant story will engage your audience in a different way and help them to really connect with you and your business.

Too loud

Loud voices can be perceived as powerful and confident but voices that are too loud and consistently loud can sound arrogant and aggressive. Make sure your volume is appropriate for the environment and vary it to add interest to what you are saying.

Too soft

Voices that are too soft are not only difficult to hear, but can sometimes sound uncertain and apologetic. When speaking about your business, it's important to use enough volume to ensure you are heard and that you sound confident in what you are speaking about.

Too monotone

Monotonous voices are boring to listen to and give the impression a person doesn't care about their audience or their message. Vocal variety is key to engaging people and ensuring your message is heard.

Too nervous

Nerves can affect our bodies in many different ways – shallow breathing, a feeling of butterflies in the stomach, heart palpitations, shaking, sweating and complete brain freeze, all of which affect the way we communicate. If you seem nervous, it makes others feel uncomfortable and may give the message that you aren't confident in your business. The great news is that you can learn to manage nerves and even use them to your advantage in your communication.

Unprofessional

Unprofessional means different things to different people and in different contexts. Suffice to say, professionalism is key if you want people to do business with you.

Winging it

If you are unprepared, there is a risk that you won't sound confident and that you won't communicate your key points. Preparation demonstrates professionalism.

Unenthusiastic

If you aren't enthusiastic about what you're saying, why should anyone else be?

Too much jargon

Jargon and acronyms can alienate your audience if they are unfamiliar with the terms. Use plain English, to keep it simple and easy to understand.

Top tip

Don't try to be too clever! I was at a networking event where someone stood up and said 'I'm Bob. I'm an accountant.' And that was it. Many people in the room already knew him and knew what he did. But his short pitch didn't tell me what type of accounting, who he worked with, what results he achieved for them, or how to get in touch with him. He may have thought his short pitch would be intriguing, but this first impression for me was poor and I had no desire to find out any more about him or his business.

Too short

The average time allocated for an elevator pitch at a networking event is 30 to 60 seconds, which is not a long time, so you might as well use it all to get across the pertinent points about your business.

Too long

Speaking for longer than your allocated time is disrespectful to the audience, the organiser and anyone who is speaking after you. Plus, you may be cut off and not have the chance to say the most important elements of what you do or your call to action.

No call to action

You may have an interesting and engaging pitch, but if you don't give me a clear idea of next steps you're missing a trick. Even if you suggest 'check out my website at…', 'come and speak to me' or 'I'm looking to connect with HR managers in the insurance industry', at least then I know what you want and how I can connect with you if I want further information or I am able to help you in some way.

Too boring

Many of the pitchfalls above could lead to a boring pitch. Boring pitches don't get results. Don't be boring.

Exercise

Think about the times you have pitched your business in the past, whether on a one-to-one basis or in front of a group. How do you think you came across? What did you do well? What improvements could you make for the future?

Have you made any of these mistakes? If so, forgive yourself and read the rest of this book.

Key points

- You need your pitch to grab attention and stand out for the right reasons, not because of any pitchfall.

- Even if you have made mistakes in the past, you can improve your pitch for the future with a bit of effort and the help of this book.

Make sure you have finished talking before your audience has finished listening.

Dorothy Sarnoff

3. 'What do you do?' – the short answer

One of the biggest challenges for many business people is coming up with what I refer to as a conversational pitch, which is a simple answer to the question 'What do you do?' It can take a long time, many drafts and numerous trials before you get it right, but taking the time to perfect it will pay dividends in the long run because once you have nailed this message it will be the core of all of your communication. You can use it at networking events, on your website, your email footer, your social media, your blog posts and articles, your business card, when leaving a voicemail message; in fact anywhere that you communicate who you are and what you do.

The reason this is so important is that when you deliver a clear and consistent message, not only does it make it easy for people to remember you but it also helps them to refer and recommend you.

I had already been working with people on their conversational pitch for a couple of years when the power of it was reinforced for me by a woman called Lois Creamer, whom I first became aware of through my connection with the Professional Speaking Association. Lois runs a business in the USA called Book More Business and one of the things she does for her clients is to create what she refers to as a positioning statement – the concept and outcome of working with you. Lois's positioning statement at that time was 'I work with professional speakers who want to book more business, make more money and avoid costly mistakes.' When she wanted a shorter version, she said 'I work with speakers who want to book more business.' I heard and read that statement so many times in webinars and on social media that now if any speaker asks me how to get more business, Lois immediately comes to mind. And that's where you should be aiming to get to with your conversational pitch so that anyone can easily remember it and repeat it.

NB Lois's pitch has been amended more recently to recognise the changing landscape for speakers and the requirement to fully monetise intellectual property. If you want to find out more about Lois and what she does, I highly recommend that you read *Book More Business: Make money speaking*.

Exercise

Think about some of the business people you know. Who stands out with a clear positioning statement? Whose conversational pitch could you easily repeat to others?

They don't care about what you do!

When communicating anything about your company it is important to remember that people don't really care about what you do, they care about what you can do for them.

Often people will answer the 'What do you do?' question with their job title:

- I'm an accountant.
- I'm a life coach.

- I'm the CEO of XYZ Company.

Or they'll mention the industry:

- I'm in the insurance business.
- I'm in the construction industry.
- I work in ecommerce.

Responding with your job title or your industry doesn't say anything about who you help, what problem they have and what results you achieve.

Therefore, you need to always be thinking about your communication from your ideal customer's point of view. What do they care about? What keeps them awake at night? What problem do they have that your product or service solves? The more you know about your customer and their needs, the more effective your pitch will be.

Your conversational pitch will evolve over time as your business evolves and you refine your offer. Mine has had many iterations; here are a few examples of pitches that I have used and the outcomes.

> I work with reluctant public speakers who want to overcome nerves and speak with confidence (short version: I work with reluctant public speakers)

This conversational pitch always got a great reaction and led to interesting conversations but it didn't help people to know immediately whether I helped blokes with their best man speech, CEOs addressing the board or start-up entrepreneurs pitching for investment. (To be honest, in the early days of my business, I was still working out who my ideal clients were – and given that I wasn't clear, it was pretty difficult for anyone else to be clear.)

> I help organisations to deliver successful pitches and presentations

This pitch is shorter and snappier, which is always preferable. It doesn't necessarily state the types of organisations; however, this kind of information could be disseminated in a longer elevator pitch or conversation. It also could imply that I deliver the presentations, which is not the case.

Some of my colleagues in the world of professional speaking have concerns about using the word 'help' as they feel it may indicate that you work for free. I know a number of extremely successful people who use 'help' in their conversational pitch and there is no question that they charge for their services.

> I prepare entrepreneurs and business professionals to pitch and present with confidence

This is more focused and gives you a good idea of who I work with and what the outcome is. If I'm at an event where the majority of attendees are entrepreneurs, I drop the 'business professionals' element and vice versa. Feedback from my clients is that confidence is a key aspect of why they come to me for training and coaching so by using that word I am hooking into their needs. It can be refined even further, for example:

> I teach entrepreneurs to pitch with confidence

What your conversational pitch is not

As mentioned above, your conversational pitch is not your job title or your industry. In most cases it shouldn't necessarily include the name of your company, although in some instances you may need to provide some additional information to give it some context. For example, if you're not a sole trader or you work for an organisation, you may start with something like, 'I'm Joe Bloggs from XYZ Company. We specialise in…'

While the aim of your conversational pitch is to give a one sentence summary of your brand, it is not your brand positioning statement, your mission statement, your vision statement or your value proposition. It's also not your slogan or tag line. However, getting clear on these will help with the process and you might choose to incorporate elements of these in your pitch.

Google 'brand positioning statement' and you'll find dozens of different templates. These can help you to define your offer and work out what you might include in both your conversational pitch and your 30 to 60-second pitch; however, the majority are far too clunky for a short response when someone asks, 'What do you do?'

The questions and templates included in the following exercises will help you to define your offer. Once you have a clear idea of what makes your business unique and why your customers buy from you it will then be a case of breaking it down and identifying the most important elements to include in your conversational pitch. The examples provided will help you to consider the different ways you can incorporate the information that you have noted while undertaking the brand positioning process.

Exercise

Take a moment to write down who you work with/want to work with or who buys your products and/or services. Instead of simply stating 'people' or 'anyone', who is it specifically?

Now think about why they use your services or buy your product. What problem do they have that your product/service solves? What is the transformation or the outcome of using your product/service?

Top tip

The more specific you are about your customer, the more effective your pitch will be.

To get really specific about your target customer, you need to dig deep. Rather than saying 'managers', try senior managers, c-suite executives, team leaders, emerging leaders, high-performing leaders, aspiring managers, ambitious managers. Rather than saying 'mums', are they new mums, mums of teenagers, stressed-out mums, frustrated mums, sleep-deprived mums, single mums? If your target is car owners, what type of car owners are they – fussy, proud, lazy, wealthy, time-poor?

Exercise

Take the information you have and try entering it into the following templates:

I/We [verb] [target market] who [have this problem] to [outcome] so that [result]

For example:

I help start-up entrepreneurs who feel anxious about public speaking to deliver successful pitches so that they can promote their business with confidence.

I/We [verb] [product] that helps [target market] do [outcome]

For example:

We've developed new protective packaging that helps drug companies deliver their products safely, securely and more cost-effectively.

I/We help [X] do [Y] so that [Z]

For example:

We help stressed out teams to improve happiness, well-being and performance so that they're more productive at work.

Play about with these templates. You don't have to stick rigidly to the structures; they are designed to give you a starting point and you may find other combinations that work better for your business.

Top tip

Use active verbs for these exercises. Here are some options to get you started:

help	supply	teach	build
prepare	manufacture	test	coordinate
develop	produce	manage	coach
provide	deliver	support	operate
design	organise	make	arrange
create	install	renovate	train

The drafts you have come up with while completing the exercises above are great for helping you to get clarity on what you offer; however, they are probably still slightly too long to be 'conversational'. So the next challenge is to reduce it down further, ideally to 7 to 10 words; 15 at an absolute maximum. And rather than being too formal, use simple language such as what you would use in a casual conversation. If you use too many business buzzwords you'll immediately turn people off rather than engaging them in a chat with you.

Make your decision on what to include based on the type of audiences you are likely to encounter, and what you want to be known for. And don't try to put too much information into it. Remember this is just the start of the conversation and you can flesh it out during a longer dialogue. You are aiming for a simple one sentence way to describe your business.

Here are some examples to give you an idea:

- We design unique events to bring small teams together.
- I help deskbound office workers to get more exercise.
- We plan weddings for couples who want the 'wow' factor.
- Our company creates custom-made furniture for awkward spaces.
- I help solopreneurs navigate the social media minefield.
- We design really cool websites for SMEs.
- I help business leaders to communicate better.
- We've developed an app that makes online shopping quick and easy.
- We keep kids entertained at parties so parents can sit back and relax.
- We match great people with great jobs in construction and engineering.
- We help small businesses to find, serve and keep their customers.
- We make birthday cakes that make kids go 'Wow!'
- I make bespoke jewellery for special celebrations.
- I help sleep-deprived mums to get more rest.

- I help start-ups to set and achieve massive goals (in their first 18 months).

- I stop small to medium-sized businesses wasting money on marketing (that doesn't work).

- I keep small business owners out of court.

- We supply innovative shopfittings for fashion retailers.

- We create cool videos for social media.

- I help parents have better relationships with their teenagers.

- We help businesses make more money through their website.

There is an argument to make your initial answer to the 'What do you do?' question a bit obscure or humorous to create intrigue, and depending on your business and your personality there may be opportunities to do this. However, you still need your one line conversational pitch to explain what you do; it will feed into your elevator pitch and it can be reinforced in all your communication.

Exercise

Write down your one line conversational pitch. Then try it out with people who know you as well as those who are not familiar with what you do to gauge their response. You may need to tweak it a little until it feels and sounds just right.

Top tip

When you speak your conversational pitch aloud for the first few times, it might feel a bit awkward. If it still feels clunky after several attempts, you may need to review the wording. Remember, it needs to be conversational, which means no jargon or fancy vocabulary; it should flow easily so that you always have an immediate answer to the 'What do you do?' question.

If you want it to sound even more conversational, you could try the 'You know how...' start. For example, 'You know how first time mums are often scared of giving birth? Well I help them prepare so they can look forward to the experience.'

Creating your conversational pitch is the most difficult part of the process and it may take some time before you get it right. But once you have nailed it, the rest of your communication will flow and you will find it easier to talk about your business in a way that helps people understand exactly what you do. This is one of the best ways to get known, remembered and referred, which is so essential in a competitive commercial setting.

If you'd like my thoughts on your conversational pitch tweet me @MelSherwood_ with the hashtags #pitchtastic #conversationalpitch.

Key points

- Your conversational pitch is a simple, clear and consistent answer to the question 'What do you do?', which can be easily remembered and repeated.

- People don't care about what you do, they care about what you can do for them.

- Know what your customer's challenges are and how your product/service helps; be specific.

- Use the templates to focus your thinking, then simplify it even further.

- Keep your language informal and conversational; avoid jargon and buzzwords.

- Practise your pitch and try it out with people to gauge their reactions, then amend if required.

- Your conversational pitch may evolve as your business evolves.

3. 'What do you do?' – the short answer

The most valuable of all talents is never
using two words when one will do.

Thomas Jefferson

4. Clarify your objective and know your audience

Once you have nailed your conversational pitch it is time to work on your longer elevator pitch, which is generally 30 to 60 seconds. In some cases you will have up to two or three minutes; however, I recommend developing a 30 to 60-second pitch first, which you can then expand. The first step to preparing any pitch or presentation is to understand what you are aiming to achieve; it's crucial to be crystal clear on your objective or your pitch won't have the powerful impact you desire.

An elevator pitch is not about selling, nor is it about telling people everything about your business. My clients and workshop participants often complain that it's too hard to explain all the different things they offer in just a few sentences. However, the point is that your elevator pitch shouldn't describe all your products or services – it should be one simple message to spark interest, create curiosity and inspire people to continue the conversation with you.

What do you want to be known for?

You need to make the decision about what you want to be known for and only include references to that one thing in your pitch. It doesn't mean that you don't offer other services or products;

you can let people know about these during a conversation or on your website. What you should be aiming for in your elevator pitch is to make it easy for people to remember you so that you don't blend in with all the other businesses.

The more you tell me the less I remember

You may have different elements to your business, or even different businesses, in which case, some people decide to have more than one pitch for different situations, different customer types or different services and products. This is much more effective than trying to squeeze everything into one pitch and leaving people confused. When you are starting out in business or just starting to attend networking events, it is important to get yourself known for one thing, so aim to stick with one pitch where possible.

Who is your customer?

You also need to be very clear about your target customer. Who do you work with, or who do you want to work with? Who uses your services or buys your product and why?

Once you are clear about who your customer is, you can start to ask yourself questions that will help you to develop a pitch that will be of interest to them.

Who is your audience?

The audience is the most important factor in any pitch (or any marketing for that matter); it's more important than the content and certainly more important than you as the speaker. The reason? If you don't know who will be listening you won't be able to craft content that will meet their needs or effectively deliver it to them.

Therefore, you need to know your audience in order to develop a pitch that will be relevant and engaging. For example, if you find yourself in the company of your ideal clients or customers, you would design your pitch to connect with them. However, you may be in a situation where you're speaking to people who are not your ideal clients; therefore, you would want to ensure that your pitch engages that audience in a different way and is easy to remember so that they can refer your ideal client or customer to you.

Exercise

Think about an upcoming event at which you will need to pitch your business. Who will be there? How might you adapt what you want to tell them to capture their attention?

Questions you may want to ask yourself about the people who will be in attendance:

- Who are they?
- Are they potential customers or potential referrers?
- What is their age, ethnicity, race, culture, gender, religion, primary language, educational level, profession?
- What do they believe?
- What are their interests?
- What are their other relevant qualities – are they business leaders, stay at home mums, fitness fanatics, gadget lovers, etc.?
- Are you similar to your audience, or different, and how will that affect your approach?
- Why are they attending the event?
- Is their attendance voluntary or mandatory?
- What role or position do they hold?

- What is their level of knowledge about you – are they familiar with you and your business?
- What do they know and what do they need to know?
- Do they know the jargon/technical terms you may use?
- How many people will be there?
- Is there someone you specifically want to engage in a conversation?

Top tip

Do your research about every audience you will encounter and, to ensure your networking is more productive, ideally you should choose to attend events where there will be a high percentage of potential customers or potential referrers.

What do you want your audience to know, think, feel or do after your pitch?

Ultimately you will want people to buy your product or service, but that is an unlikely outcome if someone is hearing about your business for the first time. So you need to be clear on what you do want them to do – it can be as simple as asking for specific connections, suggesting people go to your website and download your free report or offering a one-to-one conversation with you. Whatever you decide is the right objective for you, make sure that it is clear, simple and one message only.

It's important not to skip this step. Once you know your audience and decide what you want them to know, think, feel or do, the next step, crafting your content, is easy.

Key points

- If you're not clear about your objective, no one else will be.
- Decide what you want to be known for and don't confuse people.
- Be clear on who is your ideal client/customer.
- Research your audience so you can tailor your pitch.

"

Science shows that passion is contagious, literally. You cannot inspire others unless you are inspired yourself. You stand a much greater chance of persuading and inspiring your listeners if you express an enthusiastic, passionate, and meaningful connection to your topic.

"

Carmine Gallo

5. Craft your 30 to 60-second #pitchtastic pitch

Now that you've completed the work on developing your conversational pitch and you are clear about your objective for your 30 to 60-second pitch, crafting it should be relatively easy. Having this longer pitch prepared will be useful for formal situations where you need to introduce yourself or for more casual conversations about your business.

You already know who your ideal customer is, what their problem is and why they buy your product or service, so now you just need a few more pieces of information to develop a comprehensive pitch.

Exercise

List three benefits of using your product or service. Then make a note of one or more ways in which your product or service differs from your competitors. Finally, write down one or more recent success stories.

#Pitchtastic structure

You can structure your pitch in many different ways depending on your personal style and preference; in most cases you will need the following elements:

- A hook (to grab their attention)
- Who/what/why? (this is your conversational pitch)
- Why you? (briefly explain the benefits)
- A case study/example (recent success story)
- Ask/call to action (what are the next steps?)

Once you have developed a pitch in line with this structure you will have the foundation for a strong message to communicate the value your company offers. You can then say it in its entirety when appropriate, such as a formal networking opportunity where you stand up to pitch, or drop in elements of it throughout a one-to-one conversation. The effort you put into creating and practising this pitch will ensure you always sound clear, confident and credible when you're talking about your business.

I'm sure you're quite familiar with the way the majority of people start their pitch 'Hi, my name is…' Maybe you do it yourself. There is nothing wrong with this except that it's a bit boring, a little unimaginative and it doesn't set you apart from anyone else. At a formal networking event, by the time the attendees have heard 19 other pitches starting in the same way, their eyes are glazing over and their brain is completely disengaged. Plus, there's a good chance they'll be too busy planning what they're going to say to listen to you.

So, what is the alternative?

Hook

You need something to hook them in, grab their attention and highlight the problem that your product or service addresses.

Opening your pitch with a quick, well told and relevant story is a great way to engage your audience from the beginning and ensure they identify with you on a personal level. Stories connect emotionally with people and are very memorable.

Statistics can also attract attention, particularly if they are shocking, intriguing or invoke some kind of emotion. They can provide a frame of reference and lend credibility to what you are saying. Ensure you help the audience make sense of them by putting them into context and explaining why they are important.

Asking a question, whether rhetorical or not, immediately involves people as they have to take a moment to think. Questions can encourage individuals to participate and make them more receptive to your message, especially if you phrase them in a way that 'Yes' will be the answer. Just ensure that your question or questions are relevant to your pitch.

Quotes are another good option for getting people thinking. Referencing the thoughts of an expert in your field allows you to impart wisdom and create a transition to speaking about your own company. Once again, ensure that it is relevant. Explain how it connects with your service or product and why it is significant.

Starting with the word 'Imagine' and then describing a scenario in vivid detail is like telling a story except that you are asking the audience to create the scene in their own mind. This can be an excellent way to engage them and can be particularly effective if you suddenly change course with the scenario. For example, you might get people to imagine swimming in a beautiful blue ocean filled with colourful coral and exotic fish and then ask them to imagine the impact of three million barrels of oil pumping into that environment.

You could also try incorporating the element of surprise, perhaps with a prop or another visual aid. One of my workshop participants told me about a guy who ran a computer training company. This guy started his pitch with the question 'Have you ever felt this frustrated with your computer?' then he proceeded to drop a laptop onto the floor and stomp on it. In his pitch, he explained how to avoid that frustration by attending his courses. It was obviously memorable – I didn't even see the pitch and I'm retelling the story.

Exercise

Write down some potential hooks you could use in your pitch. What statistic, quote, question or story could you use? How might you incorporate the element of surprise?

Top tip

In his popular TEDx talk, Simon Sinek says 'People don't buy what you do, they buy why you do it.' If you have a strong reason why you offer a certain product or service, it can be powerful to include it in your pitch. For example, in my pitch after hooking them in with a question, statistic or quote, I talk about what a shame it is that so many business people are losing opportunities, credibility and money because of their inability to pitch effectively. I then say, 'And that's why I do what I do' before inserting my conversational pitch, 'I'm Mel Sherwood and I teach entrepreneurs to pitch with confidence.'

Who, what and why?

After your hook you can introduce yourself and the name of your company followed by your conversational pitch. Keep it simple and to the point. For example, 'I'm Jane Smith from ABC

Arts. We help local businesses stand out from their competition through sponsoring our events.'

Why you?

This is where you briefly outline the benefits of your product or service. Following on from the example above, you could say, 'Companies are keen to sponsor our events because it helps them to support the local community, reach new customers and gain valuable media exposure.' You may explain how you differ from your competitors; however, make sure you never speak badly about the competition.

Example or case study

A story or example that illustrates your product or service in action will bring your pitch to life and make it more memorable. It's easy to drop it into your pitch by prefacing it with 'Just recently…' or 'For example…' Then briefly explain why your customer came to you, how your product or service helped them and what the outcome was. The more real and personal you can make it the better, so include the name of your customer (with their permission or give them a pseudonym) and describe the problem and outcome in their words.

Top tip

Whenever possible, use the language of your customer to demonstrate that you understand their needs. Talk to them and find out about their challenges and why they buy your product or service. Then you can use the same words and phrases in your communication with them. It will seem like you can read their mind and they'll be so impressed that it will be a no-brainer for them to continue to engage with you.

Call to action

Like any marketing, at the end of your pitch you need to make the next steps clear. If we go back to the example above, you might say something like, 'If you want to know more about how sponsorship could help you to grow your business, speak with me or check out our website at ABCarts.com.'

Aim to repeat your name and company name and tie it back into your hook where possible for a stronger finish.

Top tip

If you are including your website address, don't waste precious time saying 'www'!

What not to say

Certain words can undermine your credibility and weaken your pitch so avoid 'umm' and 'err', and phrases that make you sound less confident such as 'I'm just a...' or 'I hope...' Avoid hypotheticals such as 'we could' and 'we can'; instead share your message in present or simple past tense. And never apologise or make a joke about how boring your profession is or how much you hate public speaking.

How long is too long?

We all speak at a different rate, which can be anything between around 120 and 200 words a minute. It's important to remember that most people will be hearing your pitch for the first time; therefore, you need to give them time to process what you are saying. Slow your speech down slightly so that you can emphasise keywords and include pauses to underline your main points. My recommendation for most people is to aim for a maximum of 130 to 140 words per 60 seconds; around 65 to 70 words for a 30-second pitch. Once you have your basic pitch script, time yourself saying it out loud so you can adjust where necessary.

Top tip

When you have a set time limit it is crucial to be very economical with your words. You can usually find alternatives, so if you're struggling to fit in everything you want to say and you don't want to lose any information, review the wording and challenge yourself to see what you can rephrase.

Exercise

Using the template below, plan out your elevator pitch. Aim for just a few sentences in each box.

Hook Interesting or shocking statistic, quote, story, question, Imagine…, etc. to grab their attention. (Your hook is a great place to highlight the problem your product/ service solves.)	
Who/what/why? For example, I'm Jane Smith from ABC Arts. We help local businesses stand out from their competition through sponsoring our events. (This is your conversational pitch.)	

Why you? Companies/clients/customers choose to work with us/buy our products/are keen to sponsor our events because: • Benefit 1 • Benefit 2 • Benefit 3 (A great place to share how you differ from your competitors.)	
Add in an example or case study (if you have more than 40 seconds) Just recently.../For example.../etc. Customer X had this problem, our product/service did Y and the result was Z.	
Ask/call to action Make it clear what the next steps are. For example, if you want to know more about how sponsorship could help you to grow your business, speak with me/check out our website at.../etc. Repeat your name and company name. NB Tie into your hook where possible.	

Like your conversational pitch, the template above is not set in stone and you can experiment with it. In a 30 to 40-second pitch, you may choose to include a case study story and leave out the 'Why you?' section instead.

If you're networking every week with the same groups, you will probably want to have a few versions and change the examples regularly. However, you should always keep the wording of your conversational pitch consistent; the more often you repeat it the more easily it will be remembered.

Top tip

We don't speak the same way as we write or read so use plain English and keep your sentences short and punchy for a more conversational style.

Key points

- Your 30 to 60-second pitch can be used in formal situations where you need to introduce yourself, or elements of it can be dropped into casual conversations.

- You may include the benefits of your product or service, how you differ from your competitors and examples of customer success stories.

- Include key elements such as a hook, your conversational pitch, reasons to choose your product or service, an example of a customer success story and a call to action.

- Keep the style conversational and avoid words and phrases that will undermine your credibility.

- Be economical with your words to ensure it's not too long.

Stories are just data with a soul.

Brené Brown

6. Weed out self-doubt and cultivate your confidence

I'm fascinated by confidence. I'm intrigued as to why people feel confident (or not), in what circumstances they feel confident (or not) and why some people are generally more confident than others.

And it's interesting that a lack of confidence shows up in different ways for different people. In my work I come across a lot of successful people who have confidence in their business idea or their area of professional expertise; however, they have a lack of confidence when it comes to standing up and speaking in front of large groups of people. Other people I know have confidence to take on new and unfamiliar tasks or make huge changes in their lives such as moving to a new country; however, they may lack the confidence to speak up in meetings or challenge a decision made by someone they perceive to be more important than themselves.

Often a lack of confidence will stem from three fears:

- the fear of not belonging
- the fear of not being good enough
- the fear of not being liked/loved

These fears are all about what other people think, but confidence really comes down to a belief in yourself: a belief in your own power and own abilities. So essentially confidence is really about our capacity to judge our own abilities; it's about the story we tell ourselves.

Having said that, one of the things I've noticed is that some of the most overly confident people I know can often be a bit lacking in ability and some of the most under-confident people I know have loads of ability; and sometimes there seems to be no correlation between someone's ability and their level of confidence.

You probably know someone who is amazing at what they do but completely lacks confidence; maybe that person is you.

So you need to become aware of how you judge your own talents and skills and of the narrative you tell yourself. Examples of some of the stories people tell themselves are:

- 'I'm hopeless at speaking in public.'
- 'I don't want to seem like I'm blowing my own trumpet.'
- 'If I sound too confident, people will think I'm arrogant.'
- 'If I speak about my business, people will just think I want to sell them something.'

Stories are self-fulfilling – whatever story you consistently tell yourself is likely to be true for you. For example, if you regularly say, 'I'm terrified of public speaking', you actually start to believe it and it becomes embedded as a belief. But it really is just made up in your mind. If you recognise and change your story, you can significantly change your life.

Therefore, the first thing to do if you want to build confidence is to start to become aware of the stories you are telling yourself then interrupt them, question them and challenge them.

Exercise

What's your confidence story? Is the story you are telling yourself sabotaging your confidence? In what way could you change your story to improve your level of confidence?

Now think about how confident you appear to others. How does this impact on their perception of you?

We all love to listen to someone who appears cool, calm and self-assured. In fact, if someone doesn't seem confident when speaking about their business, it is uncomfortable to watch and we will have no confidence in the message they are sharing.

Top tip

When you appear confident, people will have more confidence in you.

So, apart from improving your confidence story, what else can you do to both feel and look more confident?

Prepare effectively

Preparation is the absolute key to being able to confidently deliver your pitch. Preparation is not only about developing and practising your content, although preparing a relevant and engaging pitch is obviously a vital part of it. There are various other areas to prepare, which are sometimes overlooked:

- Your mind (more later in this chapter)
- Your body (see Chapter 8)

• Your voice (see Chapter 9)

You might also want to think about the logistics of where you will be delivering your elevator pitch. Knowledge is power – what do you already know or what could you find out about the event, the people, the environment and so on? The more familiar you can become with the circumstances in which you will be speaking, the more you will be able to 'own the room' and exude confidence.

Don't wing it

Rather than winging it when you turn up to events where you may be speaking about your business, make sure you are prepared and that you have rehearsed what you are going to say. Once you have crafted your conversational pitch and your elevator pitch, practise saying it out loud so that you feel comfortable. It can take a while before the words flow smoothly and you don't want the first time you say it to be in front of the people you are aiming to impress. Practise by yourself as well as in front of supportive friends and colleagues; the simple fact is that you can't get better at speaking in public without actually doing it.

Know it's not about you

Like any presentation, a pitch is never about the person speaking; it is always about the audience. Focusing on the people who will be listening will enable you to get out of your head and communicate your message with confidence. You have already researched your audience (haven't you?) so you can be confident that you have developed a pitch that is interesting, engaging and relevant to them.

Dress for success

At some stage in our life, most of us have worn an outfit that we didn't feel good in; maybe it didn't fit well or the colours weren't flattering or maybe it was simply uncomfortable. You may have attended an event and realised that your outfit wasn't appropriate; maybe it was too dressy, too casual, too thick or too flimsy, all of which can cause a different kind of discomfort all together.

One of the first steps in feeling confident is to be secure in what you are wearing. Take the time to ensure your outfit is comfortable, flattering, appropriate for the event and represents you in the best possible way. When you look good, you feel good.

You can read more about how your image makes an impact in Chapter 7.

Know the power of your body language

Confident presenters are comfortable in their own skin and know the value of using eye contact, gestures and facial expressions to connect with their audience and enhance their message. Even if you're not feeling it, people will expect you to project confidence in your communication. One of the best ways to portray that poise and conviction is through your body language. Your audience will be reading this before you open your mouth to speak, so here are some tips:

- Stand tall and straight with your head up and shoulders back.

- Use the space available and don't stand too far back from the audience (although only ever move with purpose; no aimless meandering).

- Make eye contact with individuals rather than scanning over the tops of their heads.

- Use open gestures and make them bigger if you are presenting in a larger space so that they can be seen in the back row.

- Take a moment before you speak to stand and be fully comfortable before you utter your first words; this allows people to check you out visually and prepare themselves to listen.

You can read more about how to prepare and use your body in Chapter 8.

Manage your mind

I believe that confidence is a choice. We can choose to be and feel confident or we can choose not to. If you approach your pitch with the idea that it's going to be terrible, that you hate being the centre of attention and that you're going to be so nervous that you forget everything, guess what… that's what you'll get. On the flip side, if you choose to prepare well, change your limiting beliefs and focus on giving a great pitch, you are far more likely to feel and look confident than if you allow your mind to run away with unhelpful thoughts.

As a young girl I discovered the method of choosing to 'act as if' to help me feel more confident in certain situations. One of the first times I used this technique was when I was learning to ice skate and I found myself going around and around the rink clinging to the sides. A slightly older and very elegant girl stepped onto the ice in front of me, did several perfect pirouettes and gracefully glided backwards to the other side of the rink. I wanted to be her! In that moment I realised that I would never get better at ice skating if I continued to cling onto the barriers for support. So I chose to 'act as if' I could already skate. I stood up taller, held my head up, took a deep breath, let go of the side, pushed my legs and glided a few meters. I was amazed. The more I did this the further I could go each time between holding onto the sides. I never did learn to ice skate like the other girl, but by choosing to 'act as if' I could skate like her, I was able to let go of my fear and embrace the mindset that enabled me to improve my skating and enjoy the experience.

One of my clients uses a similar technique. When she first came to me she told me she was petrified of speaking in public and wanted to be able to speak like Michelle Obama. So we did an exercise to help her get in touch with and channel her 'inner Michelle Obama'. She is now able to 'act as if' she has Michelle's poise, confidence and eloquence, which has completely transformed her ability to speak in front of an audience.

It is your responsibility to get yourself in the right state to do your best in the lead-up and immediately before the event at which you will be pitching. You may find meditation, mindfulness, positive affirmations or visualising your success to be useful practices. Sometimes even playing an appropriate piece of music will help to put you in the right state of mind.

Own the space

I can't tell you the amount of times I've been at events where someone is introducing their business but I haven't been able to actually see or hear them. This is often due to the set-up of the room: it may be that people are sitting around tables or there is a pillar or something else blocking the sightlines. Where possible, check out and move about in the space before anyone arrives so you can get comfortable in it and 'own it' when it comes to speaking. Stand up when it's your turn to speak and, if necessary, move to an area of the room where you can be seen and heard. You will appear more confident and have more impact if you don't start speaking until you are in position and have given yourself a moment to centre yourself.

I often see people give a great pitch or presentation and then quickly scurry away or sit down the moment it is over (I have been guilty of this myself in the past). Regardless of how you feel it has gone, ensure you finish strongly and pause for a moment – especially if it's the type of event where the audience applauds after your pitch. You can also use this time as an opportunity to silently express your gratitude and thank them for taking the time to listen to you.

Don't expect perfection

This one is a big challenge for me personally and I have noticed it with many of my clients. But I once received some valuable advice from Paul du Toit, international speaker and co-author of *The Exceptional Speaker*. When I asked him for some constructive feedback on a speech that I delivered at a conference, he told me I was already an exceptional speaker (of course, I was delighted) and then he said, 'Here's my gift to you: stop trying to be perfect.' And he's right. Confident presenters know that being authentic and connecting with the audience is better than a perfect delivery.

Get your butterflies to fly in formation

Are you one of those people who feels fine about speaking to a few people at a time, but as soon as you have to stand up in front of a larger group and be the centre of attention with everyone's eyes on you, that's when the fear kicks in? Perhaps you experience the physical symptoms of nerves such as sweaty palms, wobbly knees, dry mouth, shaky voice, heart palpitations and forgetfulness. If that's the case, you are definitely not alone. In fact, it might surprise you to know that nerves are completely normal; they mean you care, so it's natural to get nervous from time to time. In fact, I don't know anyone who doesn't feel some nerves before an important pitch or presentation. Even a professional speaker will sometimes feel nervous giving a pitch, especially in the first few moments until they get into their flow. But regardless of your level of anxiety, the great news is that you are unlikely to look as uneasy as you feel.

And there are several ways to get those butterflies to fly in formation.

Top tip

More preparation = fewer nerves

First, the most important consideration, as mentioned earlier, is to be prepared. Prepare your pitch, your mind, your body, your voice and find out as much as you can about the situation and the environment in which you will be speaking.

Second, one of the simplest ways to manage your butterflies is to reframe your nerves as excitement; when you think about it the physical symptoms of nervousness are similar to those of excitement. One of my clients recently used this technique as he loves roller coasters. He compared the experience of waiting to pitch in a competition to the feeling he has when waiting in line for a roller coaster ride, and he embraced the adrenaline rather than fearing it. I remember watching a family friend, Paralympian Maria Lyle, being interviewed on the BBC before her first race in Rio 2016. When asked whether she was nervous she replied, 'No, I'm just excited!' Along with her training and preparation, she used the adrenaline and her positive attitude to go on to win a silver and two bronze medals at just 16 years of age. Your attitude will impact the way you pitch your business, so if you are feeling nervous, make the choice to reframe your nerves as excitement.

Finally, taking time to slow down and regulate your breathing will help you to feel calm, centred and focused. You can read more about how to breathe effectively in Chapter 9.

If you implement these tips, you'll feel less nervous and you'll be pleasantly surprised at how confident you appear as well as how much more effective you are at delivering your pitch.

Key points

- Lack of confidence comes down to the story you tell yourself about your ability; take time to understand and change your confidence story.
- Prepare well and practise your pitch out loud in advance.
- Be aware of the impact of your image and your body language on both yourself and others.
- You are in control of your mind; practise the techniques that work best for you.
- Let go of your expectations of delivering a 'perfect' pitch.
- Get your butterflies to fly in formation with thorough preparation, reframing the way you interpret your nerves and deep, slow breathing.

7. Image makes an impact

Like it or not, people are making assumptions about us from the moment they first see us. As the saying goes, you never get a second chance to make a first impression. We are judged based on how we present ourselves; therefore, when we are pitching our business it's crucial to think about the image we are presenting as this can affect how people perceive us and receive our message.

Exercise

Think about the last time you were in a networking situation. What did your image say about you? What were you communicating visually? Is that the message you wanted to portray?

Whether you are a sole trader or part of a larger operation, you are the representative of your company so it's important to think about both your professional brand and your personal brand.

If you work for an organisation you may have a dress code, or even a uniform to ensure consistency of your branding. For example, everyone at my local printing company wears smart black trousers and shoes with a branded T-shirt and zip-up jacket.

Where there is no uniform, think about the expectations of the industry in which you work. If you are a solicitor you will most likely wear a different style to that of someone in a start-up tech company. To reinforce your brand consistency you may want to consider incorporating your brand colours into your outfit; the repetition of colour is a great way to be memorable.

Whatever you decide to wear, you need to be mindful of your brand, your ideal client and the situation.

Top tip

Ask yourself the following questions:

- Where is the event taking place?
- What time of day is it?
- What is the occasion?
- Is there a dress code?
- Who will be in attendance?
- What are their expectations?
- What image are you aiming to project?

There are several keys to ensuring your image supports the message you want to convey.

Always be occasion-appropriate and know your audience

A few years back, colour expert and founder of Colour Elements, Karen Finlayson, reminded me that your appearance is your non-verbal greeting – just as we might greet a person in their teens differently from an elderly person, similarly it's beneficial to consider modifying your look for different situations. The more easily people relate to you, the less distracted they will be by what you are wearing.

While business dress is now a lot more relaxed in many industries, choosing an outfit that is appropriate to the occasion and the attendees will help with your authority and credibility. If everyone else is in a suit and you turn up in paint-splattered jeans and a ripped T-shirt you may have to work harder to convince people why they should listen to you. Having said that, it may be in line with your company or personal style to wear something completely different to stand out from the crowd; just be sure it is a conscious choice rather than an error of judgement that makes people notice you for all the wrong reasons.

If you don't stand out from the crowd, make sure you look different

Being suitably dressed for the situation will help people to focus on what you're saying rather than what you're wearing, though an unexpected element can help to make you more memorable. If you're not an out-and-out rebel this might simply be the use of a contrasting colour in a tie or choosing accessories such as a bright pocket square, eye-catching shoes, a trendy watch or a piece of jewellery with personality.

It's important to know your own style and to present the best version of yourself. My personal style expert, Judith Campbell from Feel Brand New, advises that repetition of what works for you can become very distinctive, for example same cut of trouser, always wearing a scarf, creative facial hair, red lipstick. She suggests injecting some pizzazz into your wardrobe; you don't have to reinvent yourself, just consider learning how to add colour, print or texture that fits with your style personality.

Use colour wisely

Colour is instant – before your brain registers anything else it will register colour. Therefore, careful consideration needs to

7. Image makes an impact

53

be given when choosing what to wear to ensure that the first impression you make is the one you're aiming for.

Colour is not just a visual phenomenon, it can create an emotional response in people as well. For example, warm colours (red, orange, yellow) can evoke emotions of excitement and happiness through to feelings of anger and aggression. Cool colours (blue, green, purple) can be calming but can also create a feeling of sadness (think about the expression 'feeling blue').

I used to almost always wear black with a piece of statement jewellery or a pop of colour in a scarf, as well as my signature red lipstick. However, since I have been running my business and doing more speaking in front of various audiences, I have realised that it is much more interesting for people if I am wearing a bit more colour. It also makes me more memorable, especially at an event where there are a lot of people. Not only that but certain colours affect my mood, so if I need to get into a certain state before delivering a presentation or pitching my business I will choose a colour that supports me in that. Having said that, it is important to get the balance right as bright colours can sometimes make your message seem less credible – it's all about understanding the attendees and the occasion, and adjusting your personal style to ensure that your image is appropriate for the situation.

To get some further advice, I spoke with colour expert, Jane Chrumka from Harmony Ridge Colours, about how to choose the right coloured outfit. Here are her tips:

- Know your skin undertone (warm or cool) so that you can choose a colour that flatters
- Understand colour intensity and what works best for you as colours can be soft, muted, strong, clear, light and bright

- Create interest by using contrasting colours, for example green and purple, blue and orange

- Think about the number of colours you are wearing, for example try three or five colours as odd numbers create better visual balance

- Combine colours in the same tonal family

- If wearing just one colour, consider texture and design to create interest

- Keep in mind colour symbolism and psychology and what colour messages you are sending out, for example red can sometimes be seen as energetic or aggressive and black can sometimes be seen as submissive or threatening

- Know your audience and consider the occasion, without feeling you need to completely conform

- When matching colours, compare and contrast in the same lighting conditions

- Mix and wear colours confidently

- When choosing colours for an outfit think about how it fits with your overall branding

- Seek professional guidance, for example have your personal colours analysed

I have seen amazing transformations in both men and women who have reviewed their wardrobes following guidance from a colour expert. Knowing what colours flatter you and enhance your features will ensure you always look your best. Jane believes that colour should be a fun and creative way of expressing yourself and communicating your message. You can break colour 'rules' as long as you do so knowingly and support your decision in the style you choose.

Don't let your choice of fabric betray you

I have had the experience of wearing a thin cotton frock as a costume for a singing performance that I was particularly anxious about. Normally I'm pretty good at hiding any nerves I'm feeling and using them to my advantage to enhance my performance. However, during this particular concert I was standing under a single spotlight singing a solo and my legs were trembling so badly that my flimsy dress was shaking. I've seen examples of this at networking events as well so I always suggest that my clients choose a heavier fabric and a style that won't show any quivering if you're feeling anxious. The same advice goes for sweating; if you know you perspire a lot when you're nervous, wear outfits in fabrics that don't accentuate it. Another tip is to dress in fabrics that don't crease where possible, or if they are likely to crease and you are travelling, it is a good idea to bring your outfit to change into when you arrive.

Look good, feel good

For many of us clothes are so much more than something to cover our modesty and keep us warm. They can be confidence-boosters with transformative powers – when we look good, we feel good. You probably have garments and accessories that make you feel great, such as a favourite pair of high heels or a lucky tie. Just putting on these garments can help to change your posture and the way you carry yourself, and even change your behaviour to enhance your pitch delivery and conversational skills.

It's also important to dress to suit your body type by choosing an outfit that fits and flatters so that you feel great.

Note that your outfit should be clean and well ironed with no missing buttons or falling hemlines; also avoid wearing dirty, scuffed shoes as these things can impact on your credibility and detract from your message. Think about your overall look including hairstyle, beard/moustache or make-up and carefully selected accessories (avoid jewellery that jangles if you want your words to be the focus and not your noisy accessories).

Ultimately, it's about ensuring that whatever you choose to wear is appropriate, comfortable and makes you feel great.

Key points

- People make judgements about you based on your appearance.
- Your image should support and reinforce your brand.
- Choose outfits that are comfortable, flattering and appropriate for the occasion.

It usually takes me more than 3 weeks to prepare a good impromptu speech.

Mark Twain

8. Boost your body language

The way in which you prepare and use your body has an enormous impact on your communication. In fact, your body is your most important visual aid. When you're speaking, people don't just take in the words you are saying; in fact, you are communicating whether you are speaking or not. Before you even open your mouth to say anything, your body language will be creating a first impression. Your stance, movement, gestures, facial expressions and eye contact are all part of your body language.

Exercise

Take a moment to think back to the last interaction you had with someone. Were you relaxed or tense? Bored or interested? Happy, sad, excited, angry, frustrated, nervous, confident?

Was your body language in keeping with the way you felt at the time? Could it have been communicating something other than what you intended?

If you use your body effectively you can enhance the way you communicate by helping people to take in your message through their eyes as well as their ears. But your body language can undermine your credibility without you realising it if you're not conscious of what message it is transmitting. So the more aware you are of the way you are using your body to support your communication, the more impact you will have, both in a one-to-one conversation and in a larger group setting.

Let's look at each area in a bit more detail.

Stance

Think about a person who is nervous, self-conscious and uncomfortable. What does their body look like? Chances are they are making themselves appear smaller, with shoulders hunched forward and their head down. Compare that to a person who exudes confidence. They are more likely to be standing tall, with shoulders back and head held high. A simple change in your posture will have a significant impact on how you come across to others.

Movement

'How you stand represents the stability of your ideas and your organisation' (Fripp, n.d.). I love this quote by Patricia Fripp, international speaker and presentation skills trainer; she teaches that if you want someone to take you and your ideas seriously and add to your authority, then you need to have some stillness in your body.

Excessive movement, fidgeting, shuffling or rocking on your feet makes you look anxious; it's also distracting and reduces the impact of your message. In my experience of coaching and training thousands of business people on their pitch and presentation skills, I have found that most people are unaware of their distracting movement until it is pointed out to them. This is where filming yourself speaking and then watching it back (without the sound) can be very helpful in identifying distracting body language.

Though being grounded and centred is important for more impact, I'm not suggesting you don't move; movement can be a very useful tool for highlighting different elements of your pitch. But if you're going to move, be aware that you're doing it and only move with purpose.

Top tip

If you find yourself shuffling or rocking, stand with feet hip width apart and weight evenly placed between each leg, then very slightly shift your weight forward to the balls of your feet.

Gestures

One of the most common questions I receive in my master-classes and coaching sessions is 'What do I do with my hands?' It's strange that people don't even think about their hands in normal conversation and use them naturally to support whatever they are saying. Yet, when standing in front of a group of people to pitch or present, they feel awkward and uncomfortable. Because they're not sure what to do with them, they may find their hands are clasped together in front or behind them, or stuffed into their pockets. Arms might be folded or they may fidget with a pen or other item. These things can be distracting, or alternatively, when your hands are hidden it can give the impression you have something to hide, which is never ideal when aiming to build rapport and trust.

Instead, keep your arms and hands relaxed either by your side (which feels weird but actually looks quite normal) or keep them elbow height and gently clasp the palm of one hand with the thumb and first finger of the other hand. This has the effect of looking natural but not creating a strong barrier between you and your audience.

Gestures that are in keeping with what you are saying will enhance your communication so it's important to be as natural as possible when speaking. However, when they come from a place of stillness versus constant movement your gestures will have more impact. You can use gestures to help people follow what you are saying; for example, counting out three points on your fingers, bringing your hands together to indicate two things connecting or opening them wide to represent growth.

Facial expression

Your facial expressions will also help to engage people, especially if you smile, which is a great way to build rapport. And when you're speaking about your business, you should look like you're happy about it. I was once at a networking event where a life coach told everyone about a programme she had developed to help people find more joy in their life, but she looked like the most miserable person in the room!

When you smile, you also look more confident because it appears you have nothing to worry about. The simple act of smiling makes you feel more positive as well, which is exactly how you want to feel when pitching your business.

Eye contact

To really connect with people, you need to make eye contact with them. This is important in a one-to-one conversation as well as in a larger setting. Often people are uncomfortable with eye contact when speaking in front of a group, but avoiding it can make you appear nervous or a bit shifty, neither of which you want when you're pitching your business.

If you're nervous about public speaking it can be a bit uncomfortable to look at people when you're just starting off. I've heard people give advice such as look over their heads or focus on someone's chin, but unfortunately this doesn't really cut it. Making eye contact with people does get easier with practice so find the friendliest faces and connect with them first.

Preparing your body

Our bodies communicate a large part of our message; however, you may have noticed that when some people present they seem disconnected from their body, they simply become a talking head. Preparing your body with a short warm-up before you speak can help you to be fully present and able to smoothly incorporate movements and gestures. As we tend to carry a lot of tension, simple stretches, shoulder rolls, arm swings and shaking your arms and legs can be very helpful in easing some of the tension and getting the blood circulating, which will energise your pitch. Deep, slow diaphragmatic breathing will help oxygenate your body and ensure you are calm, centred and focused (find out how to do this in Chapter 9).

Top tip

Film yourself as you practise and, where possible, in the environment where you are giving your pitch. Watch it back without the sound to identify how much or how little body language you are using to support your message. This will also help you to identify any repetitive or distracting movements, which you can then focus on eliminating.

The way you prepare and use your body will also impact your vocal quality; you can read more about this in the next chapter.

Key points

- Your body is always communicating; make sure it is transmitting the message you intend.

- Become aware of your posture, movement, gestures, facial expressions and eye contact.

- Small changes can make you look and feel more confident and create a big difference to the way you are perceived.

- Preparing your body with a short warm-up will enhance your body language and help you to remain centred and focused.

9. Vitalise your voice

Your voice carries your carefully crafted words and is therefore a fundamental part of your communication. Everyone has a unique voice; no one else has a voice like you. And just like our image, whether we like it or not, people make judgements about us based on our voice. They might make assumptions about where we're from, how well educated we are or how confident we are. A loud voice can be perceived as powerful, but too loud and consistently loud can seem quite aggressive. Too soft or breathy can sometimes sound uncertain or apologetic. Monotonous voices seem like the speaker doesn't care about the message or the people receiving it.

When we're nervous, we tense up and tend to speak in a higher pitch that sounds less authoritative. We might also speak more quickly, forgetting to pause to allow people to hear and process what we are saying. We can sometimes get tongue-tied, tripping over our words or we might mumble, once again impacting negatively on the message we want to share.

When I first started attending networking events, I had an experience that really brought home to me how important your voice is when pitching your business.

This particular networking event was a reasonably casual affair that I attended most Tuesday mornings. I'm not really a morning person so I have no idea why I decided to torture myself once a week trying not only to get to the event on time, but with the aim of being fully awake. One morning, after hitting snooze on my alarm several times, I realised I was going to be late so I jumped out of bed, got myself ready and raced off to the event. It was one of those events that starts off with a bit of informal networking, then it moves on to a more formal part where everyone stands up and speaks for 60 seconds about their business, and that is followed by some more informal chat.

I arrived just as the formal part was starting and I joined the circle of people giving their elevator pitch. I had thought about what I wanted to say and I had practised my pitch so when my turn came I confidently opened my mouth to speak. It was then that I realised that I hadn't spoken with anyone yet that day and I had some vocal challenges. I croaked out the first few words, squawked the next few, whispered a few more. I cleared my throat several times before it finally became audible and I was able to project it a bit more effectively. I was horrified and realised it wasn't exactly the best advertisement for someone promoting a public speaking coaching and training business.

The lesson I learned that day is that I need to always practise what I preach and warm up my voice. As an actor and singer, I had been doing it for years whenever I was preparing for a performance, but I hadn't made the connection that my voice is a huge part of my brand and therefore it has to be in top condition.

Now I make sure my voice is warmed up before any event where I may be required to speak in front of a group, before any important meeting and even before an important phone call because

I know that the way my voice sounds can impact on my credibility. And it is the same for you, regardless of the industry you work in.

Exercise

Think about your own vocal characteristics. Are you someone who clears your throat a lot? Does your voice sometimes wobble or sound higher pitched when you're feeling anxious? Do people often ask you to repeat what you're saying because you speak too softly or you mumble? All these factors can have an impact not only on whether your message is heard and understood, but can also have a bearing on whether people perceive you as sincere, believable and trustworthy.

By undertaking a few simple voice exercises, your voice will be more flexible, dynamic and expressive and sound much clearer, and more confident and credible.

Preparing your body for creating sound

Before you start working on your voice, it's important to gently warm up and stimulate the muscles involved in producing sound.

Start by standing tall so that you have an imaginary straight line running from your ear down your body to your shoulder, hip and ankle. Give your body a very gentle shake to release any tension you may be feeling and keep your knees slightly flexed.

- Gently circle your shoulders forward five times and then backwards five times.
- Turn your head gently to the left, then to the right, then tilt it upwards and then forwards in a slow nodding action. Take

your left ear gently towards your left shoulder and then reverse it by taking your right ear towards your right shoulder to feel a gentle stretch along the side of your neck.

- Using your fingertips, gently massage your face paying attention to your jaw joint to loosen it up. Softly tap your face, head and neck with your fingertips.

- Open your mouth as wide as possible (imagine you are trying to swallow your head) and then squish it up as small as possible. Now try an exaggerated chewing action; then a huge smile. Purse your lips and draw a figure of eight with them.

- Circle your tongue around inside of your mouth a few times along the front and back of your upper and lower teeth, then poke it out and move it up and down and side to side.

- Keeping your lips softly together, breathe out so that they vibrate; then try trilling your tongue by vibrating it on the roof of your mouth (sometimes known as rolling your R).

Top tip

Tension is the enemy of the voice so aim to stay as relaxed as possible.

Using your breath for success

Without breath we wouldn't have a voice. Great speaking occurs when the right amount of breath passes across our vocal chords and out of our mouths. The more control we have over our breathing, the more projection and expression we can give to our words.

Some people will argue that you don't need to 'learn' how to breathe because we breathe anyway and all you need is enough breath to get to the end of a sentence, which is true. However, there are two types of breathing and one of them is not ideal if you want your voice to sound strong and confident.

Exercise

Stand in front of a mirror so that you can see yourself from the waist up. Take a deep breath in and notice what happens to your body. Did your shoulders and chest rise and your stomach pull in? Or did your shoulders remain still and the air seem to go deep into your belly?

Breathing high and shallow into your chest has a direct relationship with your 'fight or flight' response, which is the basic survival mode that kicks in when you're faced with physical danger. When you breathe here your body produces adrenaline, cortisol and other hormones and you may experience physical symptoms such as heart palpitations, sweating, shaking, blushing, nausea and temporary memory loss. Obviously not ideal when you want to appear composed and in control.

Instead aim to use your diaphragm muscles, which will help you to breathe deeper; your diaphragm is a large dome-shaped band of muscle that sits between your thoracic cavity and your abdominal cavity. When you breathe using your diaphragm, it presses down so that it seems like you are breathing into your stomach. Using these muscles allows you to have far more control over the flow of air, and more importantly they are not connected to your fight/flight response.

Exercise

With your feet hip width apart, stand tall as if a piece of string at the crown of your head is gently pulling up to lengthen your spine. Place one hand on your belly and the other hand on your chest. Focus on breathing first into your

9. Vitalise your voice

chest and then into your belly and feel your hands being moved by the expansion or contraction of your belly or ribs or both. This will give you a sense of the two different types of breathing.

Breathing diaphragmatically is a natural way to breathe; however, because most people don't do it regularly it can sometimes be a challenge to work out exactly how to do it. If you're struggling to work out how to breathe into your belly, there are two practices that may help.

The first practice is where you aim to focus on breathing all your air out and as you do so draw your stomach back towards your spine. As soon as you need to take a breath, relax your belly muscles, open your mouth and take in a quick breath allowing it to go directly into your relaxed belly area. After a few attempts you should get the hang of it (Figure 1).

Figure 1 Diaphragmatic breathing

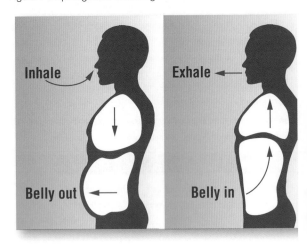

Another practice to identify where the breath should be going is to lie on your back on the floor with your knees bent towards the ceiling. Place a book or a bag of sugar on your stomach and focus on getting it to rise and fall as you breathe.

Once you have worked out how to breathe diaphragmatically, it is worth practising so that you can do it any time – not only will it help in supporting your vocal delivery, but deep, slow breathing will help you to relax, manage your nerves, and feel calm, centred and focused.

Finally, it's time to add sound...

You've engaged and warmed up the muscles involved in producing sound so now it's time to start making some noise.

- Breathe deeply through your nose into your diaphragm to a count of five and as you breathe out keep your lips together and hum to a count of five.

- Breathe in again and as you breathe out move your hum to an open 'maaahhh' sound.

- Use your out breaths to sound each of the vowels in turn: A (aaaa as in 'are'), E (eeee as in 'easy'), I (iiii as in 'eye'), O (oooo as in 'oh'), U (uuuuu as in 'do').

- Try some gentle humming up and down the scale (it doesn't matter if you're not in tune!).

- Using an 'ng' sound, slide your voice up and down the scale like a siren.

- Sing some of your favourite tunes being careful to stay relaxed with no vocal strain.

Top tip

Your voice will have more gravitas if you are grounded with your feet planted firmly on the floor about hip width apart.

Clarity

Clear diction is a crucial part of your speech so it is worth ensuring that your articulators, including your tongue, lips, teeth and hard palate, are working effectively. Tongue twisters are one of the best ways to do this. Here are a few to get you started; I recommend you repeat each one at least three times:

- She sells seashells by the seashore; the seashells she sells are seashore seashells
- I want a proper cup of coffee in a proper copper coffee pot
- Send toast to ten tense stout saints' ten tall tents
- Red leather, yellow leather, red leather, yellow leather
- You know New York, you need New York, you know you need unique New York, New York's unique
- Sheena leads, Sheila needs, Sheena leads, Sheila needs, Sheena leads, Sheila needs
- The sixth sick sheik's sixth sheep is sick

You can find more tongue twisters at www.melsherwood.com/tonguetwisters

How to use your voice

A good warm-up will help you to use the full range of expression, so let's move on to how to utilise the various elements of your voice for maximum impact.

Volume

With the potential for disruptive sounds from clinking crockery to noisy espresso machines, it is important to be heard so be aware of the environment you're speaking in to ensure that you use the correct volume. Too loud can sound arrogant and over-bearing; too soft can sound weak and insecure. Varying your volume will add interest and make your speaking more dynamic.

Pace

The pace of your speech will impact how people hear your message. If you speak too quickly, which can often happen if you're nervous, it can make you sound anxious, uncertain or insensitive to whether people understand you. Too slow can be boring, monotonous and make you sound unprepared or less articulate. You need a steady pace that is natural for you, and incorporate lots of vocal variety to engage your audience.

Pitch

The pitch of your voice is based on the rate of vibration of the vocal folds; as the number of vibrations increases the pitch sounds higher. Varying your pitch when speaking will keep your audience engaged. However, be aware that a higher-pitched voice sounds less authoritative and extremely low-pitched voices can be difficult to hear. Your pitch will also give an indication of how you feel about the words you're saying; your voice tends to rise when you make a positive point and fall when you make a negative one. For example, you would be likely to say, 'It's a wonderful day' in a higher pitch than the phrase, 'It's a miserable day.'

Emphasis

Stressing certain words can enhance their impact and even change the meaning of a sentence depending on which word is emphasised. For example, if you were to say the following sentence seven times stressing a different word each time you would get seven different meanings: I never said he loved his wife.

Pause

Pauses are incredibly powerful in speech and are a key component in sounding clear, confident and credible. Effective pausing allows you to punctuate your sentences, highlight your main points and gives your audience a chance to process what they have just heard. However, too many pauses can be frustrating for people and make you sound less credible.

Top tip

Avoid filling your pauses with words such as 'um' and 'err' as they will make you sound unsure and detract from your message.

Exercise

Practise by reading your elevator pitch or any other piece of text out loud with as much vocal variety as possible; experiment with the volume, pace, pitch, emphasis and using the power of silence by pausing at the end of sentences and to reinforce different points.

Top tip

Avoid giving words an upward inflection like a question when making a statement as this can make you sound uncertain and kill your credibility.

Tone

Tone often refers to the character or quality of the voice and is impacted by its pitch and strength. But it also refers to the feelings and emotions portrayed. For example, you may hear a voice described as having a harsh, nervous, abrupt, conversational or friendly tone. Your tone portrays the meaning behind the words.

Exercise

Try saying the word 'hello' out loud while imagining you are feeling happy. Now say it again with a feeling of anger, excitement or curiosity. Notice how the tone changes.

Now consider how often you have heard someone say, 'It's OK; I'm fine' and their tone of voice indicates that they are anything but fine!

The main thing to remember about using your voice when pitching your business is that the way you feel and, therefore, the way you say the words needs to correspond with the actual words. If you're having a bad day, or you're feeling awkward or uncomfortable or lacking in confidence your vocal tone will reflect that.

When you're speaking about your organisation it's important to sound enthusiastic, passionate and confident to really engage people and get them interested in what you have to say. But to really supercharge your communication, think about the way you feel and the way you want others to feel when they hear your words. For example, when you're describing the problem that your product or service solves, you might use a different tone to when you're describing your wonderful solution to the problem.

Key points

- Your voice has a significant impact on how people perceive you and your message.

- Take time to exercise and warm up your voice so you sound clear, confident and credible.

- Use vocal variety to make your message more interesting and engaging.

- Connect with your feelings to add depth and meaning to your message.

10. Putting it all together

Congratulations, you're nearly there. By now you should have prepared the wording for your conversational pitch and your 30 to 60-second elevator pitch. You have an idea about what you need to find out about the event and the environment in which you will be pitching. And you have considered ways to prepare your body, voice and mind for delivering the pitch.

As I have mentioned throughout this book, preparation is critical to ensure you come across clearly, confidently and credibly. There are two other vital ingredients for a #pitchtastic pitch.

PREPARATION + PRACTICE + PASSION = #PITCHTASTIC

Practice

Like any skill, you can't get better at pitching without practice. Therefore, it is essential to spend time rehearsing your pitch so that you can ensure the words flow and you get a sense of how you will come across to others.

Exercise

Practise delivering your pitch standing in front of the mirror so that you can observe your body language. Are you standing tall or slouched? Are you still or moving about? Do your gestures reinforce your message or are they distracting? What message is your facial expression conveying?

An even more effective exercise is to video yourself so you can watch it back and listen to the words. If you're like many people, you will cringe at the thought of videoing yourself; however, it is an extremely useful tool to help develop your skills. In addition to checking for verbal fluency, look for opportunities to refine your movement and enhance your vocal delivery for more impact.

Passion

Passion is the magic ingredient in your pitch; if you're not enthusiastic about your business, why should anyone else be? The positive energy that is communicated through your body and voice when you speak from your heart and share your passion for your business will bring your pitch to life and engage your audience far more effectively than a 'perfect' delivery.

Top tip

Worried about how you will remember your 30 to 60-second pitch? Here are a few suggestions:

- Make sure your 'script' is conversational; change the wording if it feels clunky and ensure your sentences are short.

- Practice, practice, practice, repetition, repetition, repetition.

- Record it on your phone and listen to it regularly.

- Don't be concerned if it isn't word perfect; make sure you know the gist and then relax and let it come naturally (don't embellish it too much though – if there is a strict time limit, you don't want to go over it).

- If you really need to, you can always have a few notes on a card until you become more familiar and comfortable with it (if you attend regular networking sessions you'll have more opportunities to perfect it at future events).

Ready, set, test

Once you feel ready, it's time to try out your pitches with other people. You may want to test them out on family and friends first so you can ensure your message is clear and you get used to speaking in front of an audience. However, the only way you're truly going to know if your conversational pitch is fit for purpose is to use it the very next time someone asks the question, 'What do you do?' Then look for opportunities to drop your 30 to 60-second pitch into the conversation or try it out at an event where you are required to stand up and say a few words about yourself and your business.

You should get an idea of the effectiveness of your pitch based on the response from whoever you're speaking with, but if you're not sure, ask for feedback about how it can be improved. Your pitch is not static; it can always be further developed and refined as you go along.

Your pitch is only the beginning

Whether you use your conversational pitch or your 30 to 60-second pitch, remember that the aim is to start a discussion. When the conversation continues and you connect with people that may lead to referrals or them becoming your customer, make sure you nurture the relationship. If you say you'll phone them or send them an email, do it. People generally don't buy from you based on your initial pitch so follow-up is the key to securing new business.

You've probably heard of the phrase 'people buy people' so when you have the opportunity to talk about your business it's important to be yourself, the best version of you. By preparing well, practising sufficiently and sharing your passion for what you do in a way that interests people, you'll be well on your way to delivering your #pitchtastic pitch clearly, confidently and credibly.

References

Creamer, L. (2017) *Book More Business: Make money speaking.* Silver Tree Publishing.

Fripp, P. (n.d.) 'Stand still – the interesting truth about movement'. Available at: http://www.fripp.com/stand-still/

Leigh, A. and Maynard, M. (2003) *The Perfect Presentation.* Random House Business.

Pink, D.H. (2012) *To Sell is Human: The surprising truth about persuading, convincing and influencing others.* Riverhead Books.

Sinek, S. (2009) *How great leaders inspire action.* TEDx talk. Available at: https://www.ted.com/talks/simon_sinek_how_great_leaders_inspire_action

Stevens, A. and du Toit, P. (2013) *The Exceptional Speaker.* Congruence Press.

If you can't explain it simply, you don't
understand it well enough.

Albert Einstein

About the author

Mel Sherwood is a pitch and presentation specialist on a mission to help ambitious entrepreneurs and business professionals to take centre stage, embrace the spotlight and present clearly, confidently and credibly. After seeing so many business people doing themselves a disservice through ineffective pitches and presentations (or avoiding public speaking completely), Mel felt compelled to share the tips she has learned over a lifetime of being on stage.

Through her interactive keynotes, masterclasses, workshops and coaching she reveals valuable tools and techniques that support individuals and organisations to design and deliver winning pitches and presentations.

Clients include large government organisations such as Scottish Enterprise and Scottish Development International, SMEs from advertising agencies to software companies, as well as individuals who attend her popular public courses and one-to-one coaching sessions.

An Australian who has called Edinburgh home since 2006, Mel is the current President of the Professional Speaking Association UK and Ireland (Scotland Region). She is a multi-award winning speaker and a qualified trainer, mediator and NLP Practitioner.

About the author

Combining over 20 years' experience in business with a background as an actor, presenter and singer, she loves helping her clients to transform their lives and businesses through improved communication skills.

For more information visit melsherwood.com, connect with her on LinkedIn, follow @MelSherwood_ on Twitter, or email mel@melsherwood.com

Other Authority Guides

The Authority Guide to
Creating Brand Stories that Sell:
Smart and simple strategies to make
your business irresistible

Jim O'Connor

The business with the best brand story wins. Find out how to write yours.

Connect with your customers and make your business impossible to resist using this sharp, practical *Authority Guide* that will save you time, money and frustration. Combine psychology, creativity, logic and emotion expertly into a brand story that will make your business stand out from the crowd. And using Jim O'Connor's hard-won knowledge and vast experience give your business the focus, affinity, distinction and competitive advantage it needs to succeed and thrive.

We hope that you've enjoyed reading this *Authority Guide*. Titles in this series are designed to offer highly practical and easily-accessible advice on a range of business, leadership and management issues.

We're always looking for new authors. If you're an expert in your field and are interested in working with us, we'd be delighted to hear from you. Please contact us at commissioning@suerichardson.co.uk and tell us about your idea for an *Authority Guide*.